A gift from Philip Rhys
Adams, director of Cincinnati
Art Museum. October 17, 1950

A gift from Philip Rhys
Adams, director of Cincinnati
Art Museum. October 17, 1950

A Memorial Exhibition

Photograph by Edward Weston

Walt Kuhn

1877-1949

Cincinnati Art Museum 1960

Foreword

The Cincinnati Art Museum gratefully acknowledges the generosity of the many lenders to this memorial exhibition and the many people throughout the country who have helped in one valuable way or another. They are too numerous to mention by name, but above all the Museum thanks the artist's wife and daughter, Vera and Brenda Kuhn, who gave their gracious consent to the enterprise and who have collaborated enthusiastically in its actual realisation. The chronology of her father's life, with its dates confirmed from original sources, is the work of Miss Brenda Kuhn. Special thanks go to Governor and Mrs. William Averell Harriman who initiated the memorial idea with a precursor of this exhibition under their patronage in Albany in 1958. Mr. Maynard Walker, dealer-representative of the Kuhn Estate, and in whom the artist reposed the greatest confidence, gave untold hours of detailed, often drudging support. The Museum also thanks the generous donors of color plates: Governor and Mrs. Harriman, Mr. and Mrs. Otto L. Spaeth, Miss Brenda Kuhn, Mr. Maynard Walker, the Kuhn Estate, Knoedler's, Incorporated, and the editors of ARTS; and also the lenders of color plates: the editors of TIME MAGAZINE, LIFE MAGAZINE, and the ART NEWS.

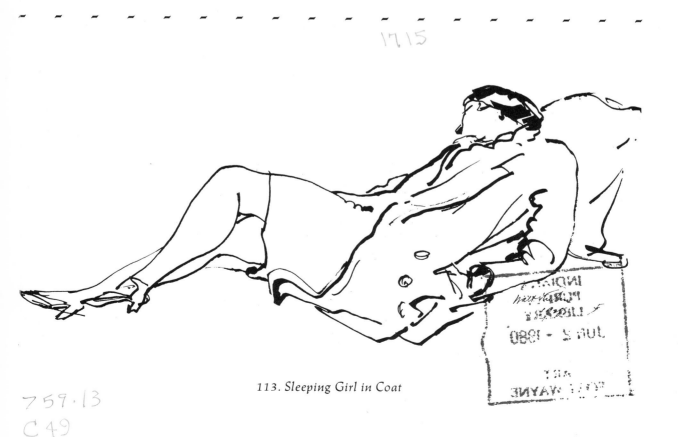

113. Sleeping Girl in Coat

An Introduction to the Artist

This memorial exhibition could well have two sub-titles. One might be "Walt Kuhn, an American Artist" and the other, "Walt Kuhn, an Artist in America." The artist himself would probably have accepted both of them while preferring the latter. Rembrandt after all could not escape being a Dutchman of the seventeenth century—these local traits flavored his whole work—but his stature as a world figure is decidedly more important. Walt Kuhn never lost sight of this first principle and in one of his many aphorisms, whose compilation would be an excellent *Guide for the Young Artist* anywhere, he said, "Ruysdael could paint a tree; Corot could paint a figure. If you can't paint a tree as well as Ruysdael or a figure as well as Corot, you're not painting." It is a harsh standard and many flinch away from it. But Walt Kuhn was inexorable, pointing out that no athlete worthy of his spikes runs against anything less than the world record; not the county record, not the league record, not even the national record will suffice. And should an artist not hold himself to standards at least as strict as those of a track-man? This may be another way of defining that unsparing self-criticism which is as essential to the artist as his daemon itself.

It is a colorful definition, and Walt Kuhn was nothing if not colorful. Six-feet tall, big-boned and rangy, with a craggy face and rasping voice—no one who felt the full shock of that hawk-like personality, with its fierce independence, will ever forget it. In his American-Artist aspect he regarded many of these attributes as definitively American and was proud of his geographic and historic location. In the quaint lexicon of the George M. Cohan era he sometimes called himself a "Yankee-doodle boy." He expressly chose as the blazon of the 1913 Armory Show, presented by the Association of American Painters and Sculptors, the pine-tree flag of the American Revolution.

Such patriotism may be a bit self-conscious, but in common with his generation, and like many Americans before him, he had to wonder what it is to be an American. And more than most he was aware of how implicitly an artist is involved with his environment, of how not only his outward style but his inner meanings are shaped by his context. Speaking of another time and country he once observed, "You can fake a man but you can't fake a period." It is a pregnant remark meaning probably that a few superficial and single traits of an artist can be copied by later imitators, but that the pulse-beat, the pace of movement and speech, the pitch of a period is peculiar to itself. Baudelaire said it differently in commenting on that gifted reporter of the Second Empire, Constantin Guys: "Each epoch has its bearing, its look, and its gesture." (*chaque époque a son port, son regard, et son geste.*) If an artist cannot escape these conditioning factors he is wise to understand them as well as possible so as to use them intelligently.

Walt Kuhn's American story is a moving one, and begins where all such stories must with the act of migration. It is a heroic act, this shock of uprooting and transplanting, which all Americans have experienced if only through their ancestors. The shock was a trauma, sometimes marring the American psyche, always marking it. Francis Kuhn, Walt's father, came alone to New York from Bavaria in 1859 at the age of sixteen. Two years later he returned to bring back his bride. Amelia Hergenhan, or Amalia as it is on the wedding certificate, was sixteen years old and half-Spanish. Sturdy and self-reliant people these immigrants, but why even a partly-Spanish bride from Germany? Daily life in the calm nineteenth century could be hazardous enough, and a by-no-means unusual cholera epidemic had wiped out the Spanish consul's family, leaving one orphaned daughter who married into the Hergenhan household. Francis Kuhn's blonde sisters affectionately called Amalia "the little black one," and a determining factor in Walt Kuhn's temperament came from his maternal grandmother.

This Spanish ingredient is highly significant and requires definition, which may be found in the clichés. As is the uncomfortable habit of clichés, they are true: the Spaniard is in fact "grave," "courteous," and "dignified." And it is the personal dignity that is most striking. It breeds a sense of personal honor sometimes extravagant, sometimes even "quixotic," a word of Spanish origin.

And there are native pictorial traits which distinguish the Spanish from other masters of western painting. One is an ability to combine the prosaic with the supernatural, to dress the miraculous in everyday clothes. Spanish still-life paintings, for example, or the homely Annunciations of Zurbarán are at once sumptuous and austere. The Spanish palette is severely limited, with a sonorous key of black, as Renoir discovered from the Spanish, after revelling in the rainbow of Impressionism only to find something lacking. He exclaimed, "Why, black is the queen of colors."

All this may seem to overstress national, racist, or genetic factors, but Walt Kuhn weighed these matters as any thoughtful man must, and pondered their application to a new cultural entity, one which had not yet entirely crystallised its component parts, asking what light they threw on the problem of the American artist. He saw a sort of historic impropriety in the century-long dominance of Parisian style and said, "How much better it would have been if American art could have grown out of Dutch painting, for example, instead of our having to fit ourselves into a French frame, which no American can ever do. And he isn't fooling anybody but himself if he thinks he can." In other words, the English pictorial genius wasn't strong enough, having only in the brief flash of Constable and Turner impinged on the main tradition, quite apart from a verbal bias and a vein of built-in iconoclasm among English-speaking Protestants. "No country has everything," he said, "the Germans are better musicians than the French, and God knows the English can write." Neither Düsseldorf nor Munich could direct the century, Italy and Holland were dormant, so Paris reigned, shaping all adaptable comers to her mold and sadly troubling those who couldn't, or wouldn't adapt.

But to return to Walt Kuhn's family inheritance; besides transmitting specific Spanish qualities to her son, Amalia Kuhn also gave him an intense love of the theater. He found the circus and vaudeville for himself later on, but his mother almost baptised him with serious theater, Duse above all. His paternal grandmother may have been Irish, which would not necessarily help to breed a painter, but could certainly heighten a feeling for the stage, in all its aspects.

After the fashion of show business Walt Kuhn dropped three years off his age somewhere along the line and his birth date is usually recorded as 1880. Actually it was October 27, 1877, and the place was Brooklyn where nine children were born, only two of whom, Walter F. and a sister, survived infancy. Francis Kuhn, immensely strong and stocky of build, spare of speech to the point of dourness, had begun to prosper as a food chandler provisioning oceangoing ships. In the 1880's, the Kuhns built the International House, a seaman's hotel, next to the food warehouse on the docks of what is now the Erie Basin. Gifts of parrots and monkeys, the talk of seafaring men, were a rich diet for a boy's already quick imagination.

He drew constantly, as many children do, and kept on drawing through elementary school and Brooklyn Polytechnic Institute which he attended in 1893. He insisted that a painter must draw as naturally and almost as uninterruptedly as he breathes, citing his friend Jules Pascin who would draw on a sketch pad in his pocket, if necessary, at social gatherings.

College didn't tempt him and he hadn't yet thought seriously of an artist's career. So he entered the world of affairs in 1897 as the proprietor of a bicycle shop. During the season he barn-stormed county fairs as a professional bicycle racer. The purses were hardly worth mentioning, but he ate, saw a lot of people and side shows, and slightly bowed his long legs. In the process he may also have sharpened his already marked competitive instincts. It was the great day of the bicycle, soon to pass, and it was still the day when an echo of Horace Greeley could be heard.

Walt Kuhn went west by day coach with one suitcase, a lunch hamper from his mother's admirable kitchen, and a new revolver. He never used it, but to be without one, especially on the outbound trip, was almost indecent exposure. The year was probably 1899, and in Ambrose Bierce's San Francisco the artist started drawing cartoons for the WASP and other newspapers, for the first time signing himself "Walt Kuhn."

Bierce was one of the few writers Kuhn read and liked, possibly because of Bierce's insistence on man's essential loneliness and inescapable tragedy – the Spanish strain? *An Occurence at Owl Creek Bridge* appealed to him especially as an elipsis of man's fate. He somewhat cynically recommended that one of his colleagues read poetry, where "you can find a lot of good titles." He didn't dislike or disesteem poetry, but in spite of his Irish genes he was simply by temperament non-literary. One stanza of Wordsworth he once said impressed him; he didn't know why but he could quote the first line. It was "One impulse from a vernal wood" which continues,

"May teach you more of man,
Of moral evil and of good,
Than all the sages can."

The last two lines sound so unlike Walt Kuhn that it is easy to understand his forgetting them. But as for the first two, Wordsworth had a painter's vision, as William Blake suggested, and the passage is a superb statement of the power of the particular to reveal the general, one of the painter's basic tools of expression. "All art is metaphor," Walt Kuhn often said, "You don't get anywhere telling a girl she has a neck like a neck. You tell her she has a neck like a swan. You still may not get anywhere, but you've tried."

The first metaphor he began to develop and send back east about 1900 was a series of vignette cartoons of birds, in their more comic aspects and consequently human by implication. A group was published by LIFE in 1906 under the title, *A Little Bird Told Me*. The captions seem sadly dated now but the drawings are still fresh and most acutely observed. He roved the west coast and on horse up into the Sierras, registering every impression a young and virile country could make on a young and virile sensibility. These western years stayed with Walt Kuhn all his life. His Christmas cards, which have been seriously collected, were always cowboy celebrations of the season, real unwashed un-picturesque cowboys, not the Hollywood variety. A series of twenty-nine oil paintings executed from 1918 to 1923 and titled *An Imaginary History of the West* was his mature acknowledgment. They are now, appropriately, in the Colorado Springs Fine Arts Center. More significantly he felt that in the west he had seen a basic America, unmachined, tough to the point of hardness, independent, masculine, but not incapable of feeling. Big with this tumult of ideas, Walt Kuhn sensed the need of formal training and in 1901 went, as then all budding artists must, to Paris.

Walt worked at the Académie Colarossi, a kind of free congress of students, models and monitors where one might or might not ask for a teacher's criticism, getting it at two-week intervals. When it came it was full-strength, no solicitous nursing of the tender plant. Young independents would drop in to work from the model and proselytise in favor of their new movements—and over all the air of Paris, stimulating every form of expression. Walt Kuhn found it almost over-stimulating; expression is the goal to be sure, but the means of expression have to be found.

So in November, 1901, he went to Munich, with its more academic stress, choosing to study at the Royal Academy, now the Academy of Creative Arts, under Heinrich von Zügel, a martinet anatomy instructor and one of the best-known animal painters of the time. After a term of this severe discipline, Walt spent his first summer of independent painting in Holland, where as he said, "Everything is arranged for you, all the colors are in tone, and the clouds compose themselves in big receding planes." And it does seem to even a much less observant eye that the Dutch painters invented their landscape. He was satisfied with one canvas, opus number one, and brought it back to von Zügel who allowed it wasn't too bad and asked for the others. There weren't any. One good canvas a summer was enough, there was plenty of time. "Time? With your puny talent do you know what time it is? It's a quarter to twelve!" He told this often, particularly to young artists. It may have been the most important thing Munich taught him.

Back in New York by 1905, he continued freelance cartooning for LIFE, PUCK, JUDGE, the NEW YORK SUNDAY SUN, and the NEW YORK WORLD. In those far-off days before the development of photo-engraving, speed cameras and other handmaidens of visual reporting, journalism was closer to the arts, not excepting letters, than it is today, and had a healthy effect on painting. Constantin Guys covered the Crimean War for the newly-founded ILLUSTRATED LONDON NEWS, Winslow Homer covered two years of the Civil War for HARPER'S ILLUSTRATED WEEKLY. They had to develop a drawing style which the engraver could quickly transpose for printing unless they wanted to surrender to the engraver's uncontrolled collaboration; and it is hard to tell whether Matthew Brady's primitive photographic masterpieces or Homer's quicker sketches are more factual

4. Flower Still Life

40. *White Clown*

in their impact. Glackens, Sloan, Luks, even to a certain extent Bellows, were spot-news illustrators, intensifying thereby their powers of swift and selective recording. This may seem irrelevant to a generation freed by the camera for non-objectivity, but seeing is still basic to all painting whatever its final appearance may be.

From 1905 onwards Walt Kuhn taught himself drawing at the Artists' Sketch Class, turning out over three thousand studies from the nude. In the winter of 1908-1909 he taught at the New York School of Art, and on February 6, 1909, he married Miss Vera Spier (1885-) a designer and craftsman in handmade jewelry from Washington, D.C. For ten years they lived in Fort Lee, New Jersey, with summers in Nova Scotia and Maine. His first one-man show was at Mrs. Davidge's "Madison Gallery," near 41st Street, in the winter of 1910-1911. On June 13, 1911, his one child, Brenda, was born.

Walt Kuhn frequently and gratefully said that his friendship with Arthur B. Davies, beginning about 1910, was the most profound influence on his career. Davies (1862-1928) was a magnetic personality with the instincts of a recluse; a masculine, almost brusque temperament which expressed itself in Isadora Duncan reveries. He organized the famous showing of "The Eight", the "Ashcan School" of realistic reporters in 1908. He could have been a great antiquarian, with a specialist's knowledge of Chinese painting, archaic Greek sculpture and other then little-known styles which he called to Walt Kuhn's attention on the assumption that a painter must know the whole vocabulary of his art and not just a single localised argot.

From that moment on Walt Kuhn became a perceptive, if unconventional, art historian, looking at all styles and periods, gleaning new ideas, judging his work against the severest standards of the past, literally "under the aspect of eternity," though he would have used no such bookish phrase. He not only knew the styles, he knew what they were "about," characterising a man or an epoch with a pithy and sometimes unprintable phrase. He would gesture to the tense thighs of archaic Greek *kouroi*, whether they were that or Apollos he didn't care at all, or for their dates or current museum ownership, but he did talk about "inner and outer explosive forces," the carved surface existing at precisely the

place where the two forces are in uneasy, vital balance; not the surface of a toy balloon but the deadly beauty of an oxygen cylinder where all the power of steel just manages to contain the terrible force within.

There wasn't much encouragement for the young, would-be original painter in this country in those days. The Macbeth Gallery, founded in 1892, was the only one to specialise in contemporary Americans, and the Montross Gallery was the only one available, at a price, to younger group and one-man exhibitions. So on December 14, 1911, Kuhn and three other young artists who thought of themselves rightly as "progressive" formed the Association of American Painters and Sculptors for the express purpose of putting on an inclusive group show. The membership grew, and Arthur B. Davies was persuaded to accept the presidency. Max Weber and John Marin had already brought word of radical new styles abroad; Stieglitz' pioneer gallery on Fifth Avenue had shown Cézanne watercolors and Picasso drawings. It would be stimulating to include these trends. The 69th Regiment Armory was rented at the not inconsiderable fee of $5,500, $1,500 down, for a one-month period to begin February 17, 1913.

Davies and Kuhn had been talking constructively about the European section—Davies found money and gave informed guidance through the whole undertaking—and in the summer of 1912 he sent to Walt Kuhn, who was on a painting trip in Nova Scotia, a catalog of the Sonderbund exhibition in Cologne, writing, "I wish we could have a show like this."

2. *Summer Interlude*

It had the largest assemblage yet shown of Cézanne and Van Gogh, most of the leading living French modernists were represented, and after a slow start it had astonished Europe. The Executive Secretary left at once, and the little stranger not only began to quicken, it rapidly grew into a Pallas Athena clamoring to be born full-grown. Kuhn went from Cologne to Holland, to Munich and Berlin, finally Paris. Davies joined him; they went on to London. Walter Pach was enlisted to help with the European end in late November, 1912.

But the story of the Armory Show, as it was popularly called, has been told many times, by Walt Kuhn himself in a small pamphlet of 1938. There were 300 exhibitors and 1,090 works shown. The roll-call is stupendous. The whole modern movement reached America in one huge leap and things were never the same again. It was without doubt the most important exhibition ever held in this country, and—Walt Kuhn used this stick to beat his museum friends—"the artists did it all themselves!"

In spite of such proven organising abilities Kuhn was never an organisation man, certainly not in either the trade-union or managerial sense of the phrase. He approved George Bernanos' statement that there are certain creatures who live by their nerves instead of their muscles: wild animals, women, artists; and who by extension of the remark should never organise. He was convinced that most artists' organisations had only an economic rather than an artistic motive, and he was a black capitalist in such matters. In answer to the artist's inevitable complaint about his hard economic lot Walt Kuhn would snarl, "No one asked you to be an artist. You're doing what you want to do." The WPA Federal Art Project particularly irritated him. He used to shout, "If they produce one good artist, just one, I'll be satisfied." He never found reason to be.

Walt Kuhn always managed to support himself, his wife and daughter, in a modest but comfortable way, spending six months out of each year in gainful occupations that had no direct connection with his painting, for which the other six months were jealously guarded. He was a kind of visual consultant, doctoring vaudeville and circus acts, even advising the Union Pacific on its first streamliners in 1937. There are many visual problems in such projects, the stewardesses for example insisted that Walt Kuhn

Drawing of Walt Kuhn by Jules Pascin

rule on the color of their nylons. In 1921-23 he made several try-out tours with Raymond Hitchcock, pointing and sharpening the acts, notably in "Hitchy-Koo."

In the wake of the Armory Show a generation of painters excitedly began experimenting with collages, dissecting Cubism and the Expressionists, becoming Fauves overnight. Walt Kuhn was no exception. *Under the Parasol* and *Summer Interlude*, both of 1910, show him to have been a competent performer in the prevailing Impressionist mode. *Polo Game* of 1915 however is post-Armory Show and definitely Post-Impressionist in its briskly decorative evocation of Dufy and the School of Paris, while *Flower Still-life* of 1918 is as charmingly sophisticated as any Fauve painting on either side of the Atlantic. And in the same Fauve vein Walt Kuhn paid his tribute to the American west in the *Imaginary History* of 1918 to 1923. Here there are recollections of Guys as well as the wit and skill of modern Paris. It is no wonder that Pascin and Kuniyoshi admired the series. It also shows his historic knowledge of military uniforms, which was put to more monumental use in the costumes of his later show girls. (Kuhn sometimes commented on the sure way military uniforms reveal a people's personality—the operatic swagger of *Bersaglieri* feathers, the square-toed, square-shouldered efficiency of the Germans, the Gallic dash under the *poilu's* sloppiness, the English officer always the well-dressed gentleman, the American somewhat feebly copying the English while remaining essentially civilian.) *Girl in White Chemise* dates from about 1920 and is probably the best of the post-Armory Show canvases the artist permitted to survive, though *Tragic Comedians* of 1922 had enough Expressionist drive to pass the test, and *Sleeping Girl* of the same year won its stamp of approval.

The *Girl in White Chemise* belonged to John Quinn, who gave legal and financial aid to the Armory Show and who, with Walt Kuhn as Art Advisor from 1912 to 1920, built one of the pioneer modern collections, later dispersed. Kuhn and Davies also advised Miss Lillie Bliss, whose collection was the nucleus of the Museum of Modern Art.

Walt Kuhn played this significant role unofficially for many collectors, large and small, and when Mrs. William Averell Harriman decided in 1930 to start a 57th Street gallery, Kuhn, who was a friend to two generations of the family, was asked to counsel and advise. Behind the scenes, and until public affairs distracted the Harrimans' interest in 1942, he guided one of the most successful and distinguished exhibition and buying programs in the country. It provided him with his own showplace and privileged access to important patrons. Walt Kuhn made and kept influential friends. He had a showman's touch in promoting his own work, which was fortunate, since he not only and characteristically refused to join a dealer's stable but would have no dealer at all, to tell him what to do. Walt Kuhn was an integer and integrated with no group or person. This could be a dangerous condition except for the saving fact of surgical self-criticism; he annually reviewed his output, invariably destroying the major part. He consistently bought back and condemned early paintings, only occasionally keeping a photographic record.

In 1927-28 he taught one season at the Art Students' League and abandoned formal teaching. It took valuable energy and had some hint of competing for student favor. Over the years he picked a few private pupils, charging them nothing except the hard price of being driven mercilessly. Not many disciples, and they had to be that, flourished in the magnetic field of so intense a personality.

Suddenly, in 1925, it was a quarter to twelve. A stomach ulcer was nearly fatal, and Walt Kuhn woke from the shock to realise that he had no passport to posterity, not one single, fully achieved absolute painting, nothing as he said that the charwoman wouldn't sweep out of a deserted studio. This was quite a test, to command the charwoman's recognition and at the same time answer to the sophisticates. But most true works will do so. Gauguin for one said that, "Nothing so resembles a daub as a masterpiece." And one time in Derain's studio while looking at the intellectual Frenchman's paintings Walt Kuhn asked to see some *pompiers*, buckeyes, *Kitsch*, popular showpieces which in Derain's hands would also be skillful professional performances. (Its etymology is obscure but *pompier* seems first to have been used derisively of mid-nineteenth century Salon pieces thronging with classical heroes whose helmets resembled the brass headgear of the Paris fire department.) Derain answered, "Ah, but *pompiers* are hard to paint."

Taking counsel with his always loyal family he decided to drop every other activity for the two years his savings allowed and with a kind of now-or-never concentration try to pour all he had lived, learned and felt onto canvas. Immediately the great symbols appeared, the metaphors: show girls, acrobats, clowns, undramatic landscapes, still-life compositions of prosaic subjects. They were in the grand tradition; Watteau and Tiepolo drew symbols of the eighteenth century from the "little world" of the theater, as did Daumier, Degas and Toulouse-Lautrec from the cabarets and circuses of their nineteenth century. What might their immediate imagery be? Are they symbols, somewhat hectic and limited symbols, of mere entertainment or escape, or are they weighted with profound human meaning?

There are many answers. Acrobats are aristocrats of their own kind. They are hired entertainers to be sure, but products of a life-time discipline, among the last inheritors of the craft tradition. The acrobats who posed for Walt Kuhn accepted him as one of their own, recognising the discipline and dedication of his craft. Clowns are conventionally tragic or at least pathetic symbols, broken-hearted under their motley, but serious athletic training and highly stylised pantomime go into professional clowning. Show girls, too, tricked out in fantastic costumes and hidden behind impersonal masks of make-up, could speak of thwarted human dignity, or more nobly for a human dignity capable of surmounting the insolence of circumstance, the impertinence of "things" As for the objects of still-life, Chardin painted rabbits probably not so much from a compulsive love of rabbits as from the conviction that anything possessing shape and color can symbolise the human visual experience in all its implications; that the extent to which it is made to do so is the proof of an artist. In landscape painting a man's attitude towards nature is implicity declared, and even the most imitative copyist of natural appearances must make the look of a tree, which is only a part, serve for the whole of its being. This after all is a device of rhetoric.

In 1927 Walt Kuhn felt ready for his first large exhibition, at the Grand Central Galleries, and by 1929 the *White Clown* had been painted. *Mallards, Hare and Hunting Boots, Athlete* and *Pine on a Knoll*, all painted between 1925 and 1930, support the *White Clown* in proving that the artist had achieved his first announced goal, that of the unadorned direct statement, almost blunt in its finality.

In achieving it Walt Kuhn revealed the central paradox of his style—he had to fight against his dexterity and his taste, strange enemies for an artist. But he felt that he had at least to turn his back on their attractions in order to control them and put them to work for a larger purpose, never "painting for the sake of painting," if such a thing is even theoretically possible. His drawings, and drawings are always the most intimate glimpse of an artist's personality, show how strong the enemy was. In them he is a true heir of the dominant French tradition, which so constantly remembers its eighteenth century. The fastidious sensuality of Kuhn's reclining figures is worthy of Fragonard or Boucher, not to say of Watteau himself. His landscape drawings—much more than drawings, they are actually black and white paintings—closely parallel the Chinese. Not that they derive in any way from the oriental, but they show a striking similarity to a Chinese poet-painter's feeling for rocks, trees, cool-breathing streams. A lesser man would have been content to build a career on such technical mastery.

This conscious civil war ended in the mid-thirties after an extended experiment with what Walt Kuhn called "arbitrary color," clashing, dissonant hues put together at their most intense, as they are in the stripes of a Roman sash. Not many of these canvases were kept, but the experiment produced one of the most richly charged palettes in modern painting. Walt was interested to discover that Renoir had gone through a similar investigation in his "dry style" of the mid-eighties. Renoir's gentler temperament quickly retreated, but the blunt earth-reds of his later work, from 1903 on, are a far cry from the surface shimmer of his Impressionist style.

If the grace of drawing and the allurement of color could be subtly weakening by their very pleasure, as Kuhn felt they had weakened Matisse and Derain, it was also imperative to see things freshly, to resist the tempting impulse to make slight variations on an artistic or financial success, a seduction often practised by dealers on rising artists. As a result of Walt Kuhn's resistance, and in spite of his self-limited range of subject matter, each of his canvases is an independent, individual arrival. Walt Kuhn took a patriotic satisfaction from this as he ironically credited the nineteenth century French with inventing "mass production" in painting, and their twentieth century successors with developing it to astronomical extremes.

He had many ways of preserving his freshness of seeing. He sought out the startling color-and-texture combinations of burlesque shows and carnivals, always in "bad taste" but sometimes reaching such heights of vital vulgarity that they became convincing. He rarely arranged his still-life objects himself, asking someone else to do it so that he might possibly be surprised by a new and revealing aspect of these familiar things. He often let his show girl models pick their own costumes from the large but simply-made wardrobe he kept on hand. The clowns and acrobats usually found their own natural attitudes, as in the case of his one big figure composition *Trio* when the three models, who had worked individually for him before, asked him how he wanted them to pose. The painter knew a moment of panic, since it was a new undertaking for him, and he wasn't quite sure. He asked them how they felt like posing, and with a brisk "hup!" from Mario, the center figure, the Act and the painting were ready to begin.

The 1930's were Kuhn's most productive period and show a steadily growing authority. In 1940 he reviewed his work to date in a book of plates, *50 Paintings by Walt Kuhn*. In the captions and through his author-editor, Paul Bird, the artist made his only published comments on his style and its content. They are often oblique, since he was speaking in words of ideas and things which simply do not exist in words, but many of them are worth pondering. *Hare and Hunting Boots* "has that strange loneliness of men without women." In *Mallards* "the line of design is constantly yielding, for the painting is really a caress to the soft plumage of these wild fowl." *The Clown with Black Wig* is "built on a linear theme of bow-knot designs. Constant repetition and variation of the theme done in a lazy, swinging tempo, yet with precision." *The Guide* is "A metallic grill of swerving lines and curves put together in the manner of well-attached and complimentary cables—as in a 'cat's cradle.'" The *Blue Clown* is "A revival of the sheer glory of pigment and a bouncing revel in impasto, supported soundly by a

design suggested in the falcon eye of the sitter. The theme is picked up by a rhythmic series of interlocking, tendril-like hooks that repeat, expand and finally enfold the entire figure giving him a self-embracing aspect." Of *Trude* which he considered his first wholly successful show girl he said, "Blond, clean, and striking a powerful stance proud Trude remains, as either principal or chorine, ever victorious." In *Plumes*, "think of a vase or bulb with a large, graceful flowering. Or think of a fountain with arching sprays of beautiful color." In *Apples from Maine*, "The fruit topples out of the weathered old basket and tosses about on the wavy light-blue cloth like part of a jettisoned cargo." Of *Rose Clown* he said, "At first glance a simple poster, but on closer inspection those hard edges turn into live form." *Apples and Pineapple* is, "A plate of bombs and a hand grenade!" In the *Juggler*, "the artist discovered that impending action is more exciting than the action itself. Explaining to the artist the basic principles

3. *Polo Game*

of juggling, the model sagaciously advised: 'The catching is easy enough. You've got to know how to throw them.' " In *Dryad*, "The Amazonian model stands like a Doric column with gentle entasis of design." Along these lines Walt Kuhn once remarked in conversation that, "There are some absolute designs: the shape of a violin, a Scotch plaid. You can't make successful variations on them." *Carnival Girl*, which he once characterised as "a young man's painting" is, "A song to the loyalty, independence and sheer bravery of these people." *Mario* "poses with insistent dignity as a star among the clowns." Edna St. Vincent Millay paid *Mario* the supreme compliment by buying it and hanging it over her desk. *Grenadier* is, "Today's illogic, uncomprehending elements marshalled into an ingenious philosophy of tradition." Of *Lancer* he said, "The chief interest in this picture is its definite and acute design made up of upward-lunging scimitar strokes." *Potatoes* is, "The tuber, enthroned." His proudest boast is the comment on *Tricorne*, "A lump of weighted form, the one, the universal substance of art, trying to get it makes art history. The Greeks had it, lost it; Rubens caught it, then it slipped through Van Dyck's fingers. Cézanne chopped it up to see how it is made; his followers fooled with the pieces. Here it is whole again." Only a master is permitted self-praise. And why not? He admitted his failures, he knew when he was good.

From 1940 on Walt Kuhn's authority increases. Traces of abstract stylisation evident in the earlier paintings disappear. Taste and skill are fully in the service of the direct pictorial statement. Following the artist's lead, *Green Apples on Blue Cloth* of 1943 could be described as sheer elegance, a quality he denied himself in earlier treatments of the same subject. He said that the composition of *Peaches* was suggested by peas in a pod, though the effect is of pearls in a velvet case. The sacramental overtones of his still-lifes with bread are unmistakable, but of *Loaf of Bread* he remarked that, "the knife is male, the bread female." In the calm assurance of the pink-clad *Hand Balancer* and in the frank sensuousness of *Girl from Madrid* can be seen the fruit of his experiments with arbitrary color, now no longer self-conscious. He said that the tense curves of *Bananas* came from the writhing energy of a ship's wire cable.

Roberto is the lineal descendant and at the same time the culmination of the *White Clown* and *Blue Clown*. When it was shown in 1946 it brought the highest price Walt Kuhn had yet received; it was then one of the highest prices ever paid for a living American's work.

There are prophetically tragic intimations in *Green Bananas* of 1946, *Acrobat in White and Blue* of 1947 and *Apples on a Red Cloth* of 1948, just as there was tragic prophecy in the title of his last exhibition, "Fifty Years a Painter," shown from November 8 to December 4, 1948 at the famous French firm of Durand-Ruel which was soon to close its New York gallery. In the course of this exhibition the eccentricities with which he had savagely defended his independence, and made many enemies, were gradually exaggerated to the point of open intransigence.

His last months were spent in a mental sanatorium, and on July 13, 1949, Walt Kuhn died of a perforated ulcer. On October 27, 1949 his ashes were buried in the Kuhn family plot in Woodlawn Cemetery, the Bronx, New York.

Philip Rhys Adams

Chronology

October 27, 1877: Born Brooklyn, New York (436 Van Brunt Street), son of Francis (1843-1928) and Amalia Hergenhan (1845-1914) Kuhn, both born in Bavaria. He was christened William Kuhn according to the records of the Church of the Visitation (Roman Catholic), 98 Richards Street, Brooklyn, and it is assumed his name was early changed to Walter Francis. He was known by that name until sometime after 1900 when he himself adopted the name Walt, professionally and socially.

His parents became United States citizens November 15, 1871. From the mid-1880's to mid-1890's they were hotel and restaurant proprietors and founded the International Hotel, 46 Elizabeth Street, Erie Basin, South Brooklyn. Later they operated the Kensington Hotel, Ocean Parkway and Avenue D, Brooklyn.

1893: Student, Brooklyn Polytechnic Institute

1897: Proprietor of bicycle shop in downtown Brooklyn

1899-1900: San Francisco, California, did first cartoons there for wasp when he first signed his first name as Walt

1901-02-03: Studied Académie Colarossi in Paris, and at the Royal Academy, now the Academy of Creative Arts, in Munich with Heinrich von Zügel and travelled in Italy and Holland.

Winter 1903-04: Savannah, Georgia, and Florida

Summer 1904: Munich, Wörth and Paris

1903 until Spring of 1905: 119 East 23rd Street

Summer 1905: Cherry Hill, New Jersey (now North Hackensack)

Winter 1905-06: 232 West 14th Street

1904-10: Helped plan the Kit Kat Club Artists' Balls

1905-14: Cartoonist for LIFE, PUCK, JUDGE and the NEW YORK SUNDAY SUN, NEW YORK WORLD

1905 onwards: 3000 studies of the nude in Artists' Sketch Class

Summer 1906: Fort Lee, New Jersey

Winter 1906: West 16th Street near Union Square

Winter 1907-08: 120 East 23rd Street and Savannah, Georgia

Summer 1908: Fort Lee, New Jersey, summer school there, of the New York School of Art

Winter 1908: Taught New York School of Art

Winter 1908-09: 120 East 23rd Street

February 6, 1909: Married Vera Spier (1885-   ) of Washington, D.C., in the Rectory, St. Matthews Lutheran Church, 57 8th Street, Hoboken, New Jersey

1909-19: Hudson Terrace, Fort Lee, New Jersey

Summer 1909: Blandford, Nova Scotia

Summer 1910: Blandford, Nova Scotia

Winter 1910-11: First one-man Exhibition at Mrs. Davidge's "Madison Gallery," Madison Avenue near 41st Street

June 13, 1911: Daughter, Brenda, born at the Hahnnemann Hospital (Borough of Manhattan)

Summer 1911: Ogunquit, Maine, accompanied by brother-in-law, LaSalle Spier

Summer 1912: Yarmouth, Nova Scotia, with wife and daughter

1912-20: Art Advisor to John Quinn

1912-13: Executive Secretary for the Armory Show (International Exhibition of Modern Art), February 17–March 17, 1913: New York, 69th Regiment Armory

    March 24–April 16, 1913: Chicago Art Institute

    April 28–May 19, 1913: Copley Society of Boston

Summer 1914: Grand Manan, New Brunswick

Autumn 1914: Ogunquit, Maine, with wife and daughter

Summer 1915: Ogunquit, Maine, with wife and daughter

Winter 1914-15: First Exhibition at Montross Gallery

1915-27: Devoted considerable time to etching and lithography

Winter 1916-17: Apartment on West 129th Street

Summer 1917: Indian Lake, Adirondacks, New York, with family

1917-19: Founder of Penguin Club

Winter 1917-18: Apartment on West 22nd Street

Autumn 1919: Trip with family to Portland, Cape Elizabeth, Old Orchard, Higgins Beach, Maine, and Gloucester, Massachusetts

1919-49: Resided in New York City (Borough of Manhattan)

Apartments:

    152 West 14th Street–1918-24

225 West 14th Street—1924-25

Hotel Albert, 65 University Place—winter 1925-26

66 West 11th Street—1926-36

Hotel Albert, 65 University Place—1936-49

Studios:

23 East 14th Street—1918-28

11 East 13th Street—1920-about 1926

112 East 18th Street—1928-49

Summer 1920: Canoe Place (now Hampton Bays) Long Island, New York, with family

Autumn 1920: Bought cottage at 18 Stearns Road, Ogunquit, Maine, for summer residential and studio use

1920: Exhibition at M. de Zayas Gallery

1922-1924-1925: Exhibitions at Montross Gallery

Summer 1922: Designed and directed numbers for acts for Michio Ito's "Pinwheel" Revue, Earl Carrol Theatre

1923: Designed and directed numbers for acts for "Hitchy-Koo" Revue with Raymond Hitchcock

Winter 1922-23: Designed and directed number for "Lilies of the Field" pantomime at Strand Theater. Act also played three theaters in Chicago

Autumn 1923: Designed and directed numbers for "Forty-niners" Revue. "Music Ride" Act from there at Strand Theater, Christmas Week

1925: Suffered stomach ulcer which was treated medicinally

Summer 1925: France, Germany, Austria, Holland, England, with family

Winter 1925-26: Designed and directed numbers for acts in Dietz and Ryskind "Merry-go-Round" Revue

1927: Exhibition at Grand Central Galleries

Winter 1927-28: Taught at the Art Students' League

Summer 1928: Prescott, Arizona, and San Francisco, California with family

1930-42: Exhibited at the Marie Harriman Gallery

Spring 1931: Spain, Belgium, Germany, Switzerland, France

Spring 1933: Portugal and France with family

1936-41: In Chicago, Colorado, Sun Valley and California various times in connection with work for Union Pacific Railroad; official title, "Consulting Architect"

Summer 1936: Designed "Frontier Shack" Club Car for Streamliner "City of Denver," route between Chicago and Denver

Summer 1937: Designed "Little Nugget" Club Car for Streamliner "City of Los Angeles," route between Chicago and Los Angeles

1941: Designed decorative panels for "Hollywood" Club Car for Streamliner "City of Los Angeles"

January-February 1947: Hobe Sound and Stuart, Florida

1941-48: Press Pass to Ringling Brothers-Barnum and Bailey Circus when performing at Madison Square Garden

February 1948: Sarasota, Florida, circus winter headquarters

April 1948: Colorado and California

June 1948: Fulfilled his life-long dream of buying a Cape Cod cottage type house, five miles south of Ogunquit, Maine, on River Road, Cape Neddick. He had saved money inherited from his father in 1928 to use for such a purpose.

September 1948: Stayed in Cape Neddick house, which he planned to use from April to October of each year; was contemplating closing his New York studio and bringing its contents to Maine where he looked forward to painting landscapes

November 8–December 4, 1948: Last exhibition, "Fifty Years a Painter" at Durand-Ruel Gallery

November 25, 1948: Stricken with a nervous breakdown

July 13, 1949: Died at New York Hospital, Westchester Division, White Plains, New York, very suddenly from perforated stomach ulcer

October 27, 1949: Ashes interred in the Kuhn family plot in Woodlawn Cemetery, Bronx, New York

70. Trees—Vermont

71. Trio

Catalog

OIL PAINTINGS

1 Under the Parasol
about 1910, height 24″ width 20″
lent by the Kuhn Estate

2 Summer Interlude
about 1910, height 30″ width 43″, illustrated
lent by the Kuhn Estate

3 Polo Game
about 1915, height 25″ width 30″, illustrated
lent by the Kuhn Estate

4 Flower Still Life
about 1918, height 35″ width 20″,
reproduced in color
lent by the Kuhn Estate

5 Girl in White Chemise
about 1920, height 30″ width 25″, illustrated
lent by the Kuhn Estate

6 Tragic Comedians
1922, height 95″ width 45″
lent by Mr. Joseph H. Hirshhorn, New York

7 Sleeping Girl
about 1922, height 54″ width 42″
lent by the Museum of Art of Ogunquit, Maine

IMAGINARY HISTORY OF THE WEST
lent by the Colorado Springs Fine Arts Center,
Colorado
gift of Vera and Brenda Kuhn

8 Aborigine
1918, height 9½″ width 5¾″

9 Attack on the Stage Coach
1918, height 14″ width 19″

10 Combat
1918, height 11½″ width 17½″

11 Commissioners
1918, height 9¾″ width 15¾″

12 Defending the Blockhouse
1918, height 10″ width 13″

13 Indian Lore
1918, height 8½″ width 12½″

14 Indians and Cavalry
1918, height 9¾″ width 13″

15 Pequod
1918, height 12″ width 17″

16 Pow-Wow No. 1
1918, height 9¾″ width 15¾″

17 Pow-Wow No. 2
1918, height 12″ width 16″

18 The Messenger
1918, height 12″ width 16″

19 The Young Chief
1918, height 9¾″ width 14″, illustrated

20 Three Indians
1918, height 8″ width 14″

21 Warrior
1918, height 10″ width 12¾″

22 Cavalry Outpost
1919, height 10″ width 15¾″

23 Imaginary History
1919, height 12″ width 15″

24 Medicine
1919, height 8¼″ width 10″

25 Mining Camp
1919, height 12″ width 17″

26 Vigilantes
1919, height 4¾″ width 6¾″

27 Wild West No. 1
1919, height 16″ width 20″

28 The Long Horn Saloon
1919, height 20″ width 24″

29 Western Cafe
1919, height 20″ width 24″

30 Bar Room Fight
1919, height 9¾″ width 10¾″

31 Indian Raid
1920, height 9″ width 10¾″

32 The Council Table
1920, height 16″ width 20″, illustrated

33 Indian Fighters
    1923, height 9″ width 13″, illustrated

34 Ambushed Horseman
    Undated, height 8″ width 11″

35 Indians Attacking Covered Wagon
    Undated, height 12½″ width 15″

36 Wild West No. 2
    Undated, height 12½″ width 15″

37 Mallards
    1926, height 32″ width 24″
    lent by the Detroit Institute of Arts, Michigan

38 Hare and Hunting Boots
    1926, height 29″ width 27″, illustrated
    lent by Mr. & Mrs. William Averell Harriman,
    New York

39 Portrait of Brenda
    1927, height 15″ width 12″, illustrated
    lent by the Kuhn Estate

40 White Clown
    1929, height 40″ width 30″,
    reproduced in color
    lent by Mr. & Mrs. William Averell Harriman,
    New York

41 Pine on a Knoll
    1929, height 25″ width 30″, illustrated
    lent by Mr. & Mrs. William Averell Harriman,
    New York

42 Athlete
    1929, height 20″ width 24″
    lent by the Jewett Art Museum,
    Wellesley College, Massachusetts

43 Clown with Black Wig
    1930, height 40″ width 30″, illustrated
    lent by the Metropolitan Museum of Art,
    New York
    George A. Hearn Fund, 1956

44 The Man from Eden
    1930, height 30″ width 25″, illustrated
    lent by the Albright Art Gallery,
    Buffalo, New York

45 Acrobat with Cigarette
    1930, height 24″ width 20″
    lent by the Kuhn Estate

46 Clown with Red Wig
    1931, height 30″ width 36″, illustrated
    lent by Mr. and Mrs. Otto L. Spaeth,
    New York

47 Plumes
    1931, height 40″ width 30″
    lent by Phillips Gallery, Washington, D.C.

48 The Guide
    1931, height 24″ width 20″, illustrated
    lent by the University of Nebraska Art
    Galleries, Lincoln, Nebraska

49 Trude
    1931, height 68″ width 33¼″, illustrated
    lent by the Santa Barbara Museum of Art,
    California

50 Top Man
    1931, height 72″ width 32″
    lent by the Kuhn Estate

51 Blue Clown
    1931, height 30″ width 25″, illustrated
    lent by the Whitney Museum of American
    Art, New York

52 Rose Clown
    1932, height 24″ width 20″
    lent by the Kuhn Estate

53 Apples from Maine
    1932, height 40″ width 30″
    lent by the Metropolitan Museum of Art,
    New York
    George A. Hearn Fund, 1950

54 Young Clown
    1932, height 30″ width 25″
    lent by the Denver Art Museum, Colorado

55 Apples in the Hay
    1932, height 30″ width 40″, illustrated
    lent by the Museum of Modern Art,
    New York
    given anonymously

56 Miss X
    1932, height 30″ width 25″
    lent by the Kuhn Estate

57 Apples and Pineapple
    1933, height 25″ width 30″, illustrated
    lent by Mr. & Mrs. William Averell Harriman,
    New York

58 Apples
1933, height 20″ width 24″
lent by Mr. and Mrs. S. A. Davidson,
Scranton, Pennsylvania

59 Three Apples
1933, height 8″ width 10″
lent by Mr. and Mrs. Gregory Doherty,
Tarrytown, New York

60 Zinnias
1933, height 25″ width 30″, illustrated
lent by Mr. & Mrs. William Averell Harriman,
New York

61 Juggler
1934, height 30¼″ width 25½″, illustrated
lent by the William Rockhill Nelson Gallery
of Art, Kansas City, Missouri

62 Athlete in White Face
1934, height 40″ width 30″
lent by the Kuhn Estate

63 Apples with Leaves
1934, height 15½″ width 12½″
lent by Mrs. Charles S. Payson, New York

64 Apples in Bowl
1934, height 25″ width 30″
lent by Mr. and Mrs. Harry Daniel,
Bristol, Tennessee

65 Dryad
1935, height 34″ width 23″, illustrated
lent by the Kuhn Estate

66 Clown with Mandolin
1935, height 20″ width 32″
lent by Mr. and Mrs. Gary Cooper,
Beverly Hills, California

67 Miss R
1936, height 30″ width 25″
lent by Helen Hayes, (Mrs. Charles MacArthur),
Nyack, New York

68 Wisconsin
1936, height 20″ width 16″
lent by the Kuhn Estate

69 Carnival Girl
1936, height 40″ width 30″, illustrated
lent by the Kuhn Estate

70 Trees—Vermont
1937, height 30″ width 40″,
reproduced in color
lent by the Kuhn Estate

71 Trio
1937, height 72″ width 50″,
reproduced in color
lent by the Colorado Springs
Fine Arts Center, Colorado

72 Water Butt
1937, height 25″ width 30″, illustrated
lent by the Kuhn Estate

73 Musical Clown
1938, height 40″ width 30″, illustrated
lent by the Whitney Museum
of American Art, New York

74 Mario
1938, height 34″ width 23″, illustrated
lent by the Kuhn Estate

75 Grenadier
1938, height 40″ width 30″,
reproduced in color
lent by the Kuhn Estate

76 Moist Forest
1938, height 30″ width 40″
lent by the Kuhn Estate

77 Lavender Plumes
1938, height 40″ width 30″, illustrated
lent by the Kuhn Estate

78 Veteran Acrobat
1938, height 24″ width 20″, illustrated
lent by the Columbus Gallery of Fine Arts,
Ohio

79 Green Apples and Scoop
1939, height 30″ width 40″,
reproduced in color
lent by Mr. & Mrs. William Averell Harriman,
New York

80 Hat with Blue Ribbon
1939, height 30″ width 25″, illustrated
lent by Mr. & Mrs. Merritt Cutler,
South Norwalk, Connecticut

81 Lancer
1939, height 45″ width 26″, illustrated
lent by the Permanent Collection,
The Currier Gallery of Art,
Manchester, New Hampshire

82 Tricorne
    1939, height 27″ width 21″,
    reproduced in color
    Cincinnati Art Museum, Ohio
    acquired through the Virginia Helms Irwin
    Bequest

83 Dancing Clown
    1940, height 12″ width 9″
    lent by Mr. and Mrs. Frank Winton,
    Birmingham, Michigan

84 Potatoes
    1940, height 30″ width 40″, illustrated
    lent by the Kuhn Estate

85 Two Clowns
    1940, height 14″ width 16″
    lent by Mr. and Mrs. S. A. Davidson,
    Scranton, Pennsylvania

86 Bananas
    1941, height 40″ width 30″
    lent by the Kuhn Estate

87 Clown with Beret
    1942, height 11″ width 7½″
    lent by Dr. Arnold Emch, Chicago, Illinois

88 Hand Balancer
    1942, height 40″ width 30″, illustrated
    lent by Mr. Fred L. Palmer, New York

89 Clown with Rooster
    1942, height 5½″ width 8½″
    lent by the Kuhn Estate

90 Acrobat in Red and Green
    1942, height 24″ width 20″,
    reproduced in color
    lent by the Metropolitan Museum of Art,
    New York
    George A. Hearn Fund, 1950

91 Girl from Madrid
    1942, height 40″ width 30″, illustrated
    lent by the Kuhn Estate

92 Clown with Drum
    1942, height 60″ width 40″,
    reproduced in color
    lent by the Kuhn Estate

93 Green Apples on Blue Cloth
    1943, height 30″ width 40″, illustrated
    lent by Mr. and Mrs. Otto L. Spaeth,
    New York

94 Peaches
    1943, height 7″ width 19″, illustrated
    lent by Mr. and Mrs. Philip R. Adams,
    Cincinnati, Ohio

95 Green Apples with Gray Cloth
    1943, height 25″ width 30″
    lent by the John Herron Art Institute,
    Indianapolis, Indiana

96 Girl in White and Silver
    1943, height 40″ width 30″
    lent by the Metropolitan Museum of Art,
    New York
    George A. Hearn Fund, 1950

97 Portrait of Young Man (Sol Davidson)
    1944, height 16″ width 12″
    lent by Mr. and Mrs. S. A. Davidson,
    Scranton, Pennsylvania

98 Smiling Clown
    1945, height 9″ width 7″
    lent by Mr. and Mrs. Walter L. Wyckoff,
    Seattle, Washington

99 Roberto
    1946, height 40″ width 30″, illustrated
    lent by Mr. and Mrs. Harry Daniel,
    Bristol, Tennessee

100 Loaf of Bread
    1946, height 16″ width 20″,
    reproduced in color
    lent by Mr. and Mrs. Otto L. Spaeth,
    New York

101 Miss D
    1946, height 26″ width 19″
    lent by Mr. Mitchell Wilder,
    San Francisco, California

102 Oak
    1946, height 30″ width 40″
    lent by the Kuhn Estate

103 Green Bananas
    1946, height 24″ width 20″, illustrated
    lent by the Des Moines Art Center, Iowa

104 Ed Hennessey
    1947, height 12″ width 8″
    lent by Mr. and Mrs. R. L. Sergel,
    Chicago, Illinois

105 Dominique
1947, height 10″ width 8″
lent by Mr. and Mrs. R. L. Sergel,
Chicago, Illinois

106 Challa
1947, height 12″ width 14″
lent by Mr. and Mrs. Henry R. Hope,
Bloomington, Indiana

107 Acrobat in White and Blue
1947, height 29¼″ width 24¼″, illustrated
lent by Mr. Joseph H. Hirshhorn, New York

108 Bread with Knife
1948, height 16″ width 20″
lent by the Roland P. Murdock Collection,
Wichita Art Museum, Kansas

109 Apples on Red Cloth
1948, height 25″ width 30″, illustrated
lent by the Kuhn Estate

FIGURE DRAWINGS AND WATERCOLORS
Walt Kuhn's drawings are to be found in
many public and private
collections, but all those in this section
are lent by the Kuhn Estate.

110 Nude Reclining
1928, height 14¼″ width 22½″, illustrated
Ink

111 Nude, Head and Shoulders
1928, height 20″ width 16″
Wash drawing

112 Nude Seated on Floor, Right Arm Extended
1928, height 20″ width 16″
Wash drawing

113 Sleeping Girl in Coat
1928, height 9″ width 15½″, illustrated
Ink

114 Sleeping Figure, Facing Right
1929, height 12″ width 19″
Ink

115 Nude on Sofa
1929, height 12″ width 19″, illustrated
Ink

116 Reclining Nude, Facing Left
1929, height 12″ width 19″, illustrated
Ink

117 Nude Seated on Floor
1930, height 12″ width 19″
Ink

118 Reclining Nude on Striped Blanket
undated, height 12″ width 18″
Watercolor

119 Amalda
undated, height 16″ width 12″
Watercolor

LANDSCAPE DRAWINGS
lent by the Kuhn Estate

120 Moist Forest
1931, height 19″ width 24″
Wash drawing

121 Trout Stream
1931, height 19″ width 24″, illustrated
Wash drawing

122 Black Pine
1932, height 24″ width 19″
Wash drawing

123 Canoe Birches
1934, height 19″ width 24″
Wash drawing

124 Falls in the Catskills
1935, height 19″ width 24″
Wash drawing

125 Rock Formation
1936, height 19″ width 24″, illustrated
Wash drawing

126 Island, Golden Gate Park
1936, height 19″ width 24″, illustrated
Wash drawing

127 Trees at Noon
1936, height 24″ width 19″
Wash drawing

WATERCOLOR STUDIES
AND DRAWINGS FOR OIL PAINTINGS
With the exception of numbers 133 and 136
all of these are lent by the Kuhn Estate

128 Rabbit with Cloth
related to "Hare and Hunting Boots"
number 38
1928, height 16″ width 20″
Wash drawing

149. Two Equestriennes

129 Clown with Black Wig
related to number 43
1930, height 16″ width 10″, illustrated
Watercolor

130 Study for Anne
1930, height 19″ width 13½″
Watercolor

131 Trude
related to number 49
1931, height 18½″ width 13½″
Watercolor

132 Study for Apples from Maine
related to number 53
1932, height 13½″ width 20″,
reproduced in color
Watercolor

133 Study for Trio
related to number 71
1937, height 14″ width 12″,
reproduced in color

Watercolor
lent by Mr. Mitchell Wilder,
San Francisco, California

134 Lavender Plumes
related to number 77
1938, height 19″ width 13″
Watercolor

135 Study for Musical Clown
related to number 73
1938, height 22″ width 15″
Watercolor

136 Clown in his Dressing Room
1943, height 19½″ width 13½″
Watercolor
lent by Mr. Fred Bartlett,
Colorado Springs, Colorado

137 Roberto
related to number 100
1946, height 20½″ width 8″
Ink drawing

138 Roberto
related to number 99
1946, height 17″ width 10″, illustrated
Watercolor

139 Roberto
related to number 99
1946, height 18″ width 12″
Drawing

SKETCHES
With the exception of number 140,
these sketches are lent by the Kuhn Estate

140 The Longhorn Bar
1928, height 9″ width 11½″
Watercolor
lent by the Museum of Art of
Ogunquit, Maine

141 Four Clowns with Banjo
1940, height 9½″ width 12″
Ink and watercolor

142 Two Clowns with Dog
1940, height 8½″ width 11″
Ink

143 The Mathematician
1941, height 9¼″ width 5″
Ink and watercolor

144 Siesta
1941, height 6″ width 10″
Ink and watercolor

145 Dressing Tent
1941, height 7½″ width 9½″
Ink and watercolor

146 Clown, Woman, Horse
1941, height 6½″ width 10½″
Ink and watercolor

147 Clown with Trumpet
1947, height 12″ width 7½″
Ink

148 Girl in a Plumed Helmet
1947, height 12″ width 8″
Ink

149 Two Equestriennes
1947, height 11½″ width 12¼″, illustrated
Ink

150 Veteran Clown
1947, height 6½″ width 5¼″
Ink and wash

151 Clown Heads and a Horse
1947, height 9½″ width 12″
Ink

152 Clown with Bug
1947, height 4½″ width 11″
Ink

153 Clown Walking Tightrope
1947, height 12″ width 7½″
Ink

154 Clown Walking Tightrope Arms Extended
1947, height 12″ width 7½″, illustrated
Ink

155 Frightened Horses
1947, height 5¼″ width 8½″
Ink and watercolor

75. *Grenadier*

79. Green Apples and Scoop

5. *Girl in White Chemise*

19. *The Young Chief*

32. *The Council Table*

33. *Indian Fighters*

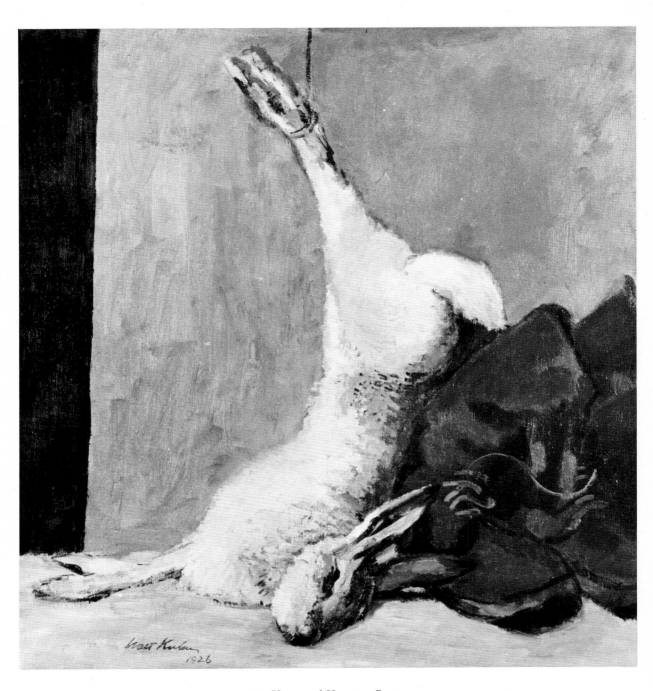

38. Hare and Hunting Boots

39. *Portrait of Brenda*

41. *Pine on a Knoll*

1715

43. *Clown with Black Wig*

44. *The Man from Eden*

82. *Tricorne*

90. *Acrobat in Red and Green (detail)*

46. *Clown with Red Wig*

48. The Guide

49. Trude

51. *Blue Clown*

55. *Apples in the Hay*

57. Apples and Pineapple

60. *Zinnias*

61. *Juggler*

65. *Dryad*

69. *Carnival Girl*

72. Water Butt

73. Musical Clown

74. Mario

77. *Lavender Plumes*

78. Veteran Acrobat

80. Hat with Blue Ribbon

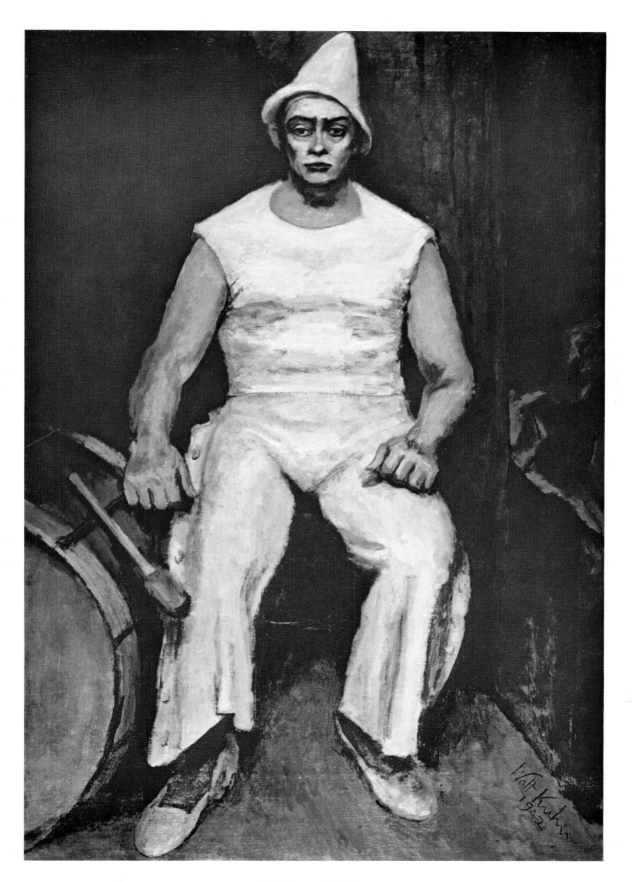

92. *Clown with Drum*

100. Loaf of Bread

81. *Lancer*

84. Potatoes

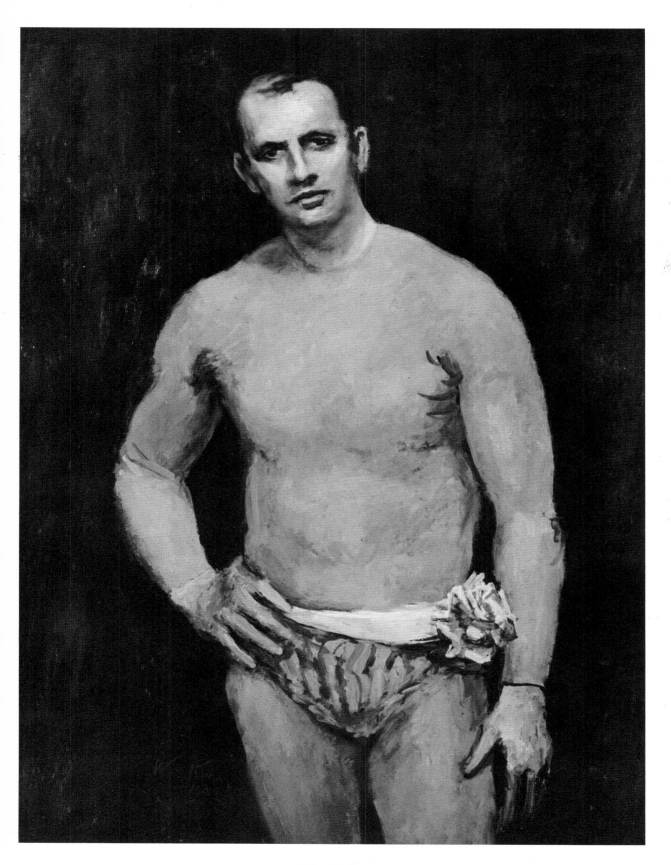

88. *Hand Balancer*

91. Girl from Madrid

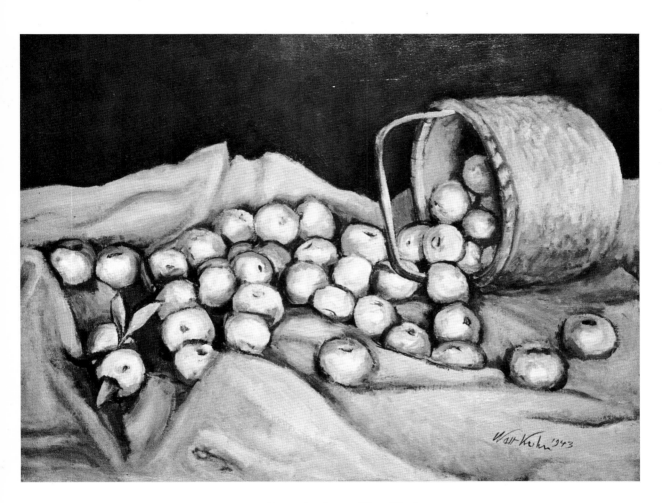

93. *Green Apples on Blue Cloth*

94. Peaches

99. *Roberto*

103. Green Bananas

1932

132. Study for Apples from Maine

133. *Study for Trio*

107. *Acrobat in White and Blue*

109. Apples on Red Cloth

115. Nude on Sofa

116. Reclining Nude, Facing Left

110. *Nude Reclining*

121. *Trout Stream*

125. Rock Formation

126. Island, Golden Gate Park

129. *Clown with Black Wig (watercolor)*

Study for "Roberto"
1946

138. Roberto (watercolor)

154. Clown Walking Tightrope Arms Extended